Captive to WORDS

UMBER PERVAIZ

AURAQ

Printed in the Islamic Republic of Pakistan.

Printed:	August, 2020
Edition:	1st
ISBN:	978-969-749-001-1
Price:	Rs 1,000 PKR, $10 US

ISLAMABAD, PAKISTAN

raabta@auraqpublications.com.pk | +92-300-0571-530
www.auraqpublications.com.pk | @AuraqPublications

CONTENT LIST

Pathetic Desires

O rich man, up high you stand,

Just give that slum a slight glance.
You've got riches, yet no peace,
He owns nothing, still lives in ease.

Huge palaces, materials...still no bliss,

Ample of real treasures you'd miss.

Sacrificed more, succeeded less,

World for you is far more as chess.

He lives in a log cabin with joy,

Holding dreams to soar beyond the sky.

But when choices risk the loved ones,

Gives away everything he held once.

Fortunes do never last forever,

Greed has neither benefited ever.

Body is clay; let the soul live,

Nothing's appealing than inner relief.

UMBER PERVAIZ

Time Pact

There's nothing time can't heal,
All the discomforts and all deal.
Days overlook and days do come,
Time could treat the heart numb.

Stronger and prevailing every day
Nothing will be left to repay.
But by no means ever be an abet,
Don't starve to be an evil's pet.

Time will certainly clear surrounding fog,
Not at all times things remain vogue.
The trends will one day change,
Someday the whole thing will get in range.

Verdicts

O man, now whom do you criticise?
If only for once, you adjudged wise.
As you choose for thou self, do for other,
The wickedness would never grow farther.

We all are humans with various rages,
Free yourself from those unseen cages,
You can snatch everything they feel,
But can never take scars...that demand
heal.

Have it all along, still you weep,
With wisdom-less mates standing in heap.
Yelling out loud for serious change,
But that's just a casual fain.

Mending My Way

Whenever I try to move on,
why do I land up in moan?
Don't know where on earth my dreams take me.
It's not in my hand; it's just destiny.
Well, all the things worth a try,
Troubles easily don't say good bye.

There's a light behind every dark end,
It's a long bridge that I need to mend.
I'll somehow reach somewhere,
Just need to pull up all the gears.
Inside every heart, there's more or less light,
You're a brave warrior, so fight.

Old scars never do easily heal,
It's just the time with which we deal.
Looking in the mirror what I see
Lets me be no one, but just me.
I have continuously battled to escape,
But every time land up in same scape.

Dead Souls

For everyone I observed is disguised,
Behind that fake smile, evil reside.
Whole lot of suffering for endangered
souls,
Feeling less dead, heart beats behind the
wall.

Observe all but turn away in ignorance,
Far past we could've taken stance.
Let them grow, laugh in their own light,
Life was never a battlefield to prepare for
fight.

For season never lasts too long,
We only appreciate beauty when it's gone.
Thou let the envy free that burden,
Thy love can thaw out the heart harden.

UMBER PERVAIZ

Free will

The breath inhaled cuts my spirit apart,
For it's just heart; stop tossing darts,
No, sir, definitely not! Don't burden anymore,
Why? These sufferings explain me what for.

It's my life expectancy; let me choose my path,
I'm not your servant; stop being wrath,
I don't demand no matter what you hold,
I'm a human, not a clay to mould.

For once, if you understood what I felt,
How deep inside that harshness welt,
You are a being, holding feeling,
Why don't you get what I am dealing?

Mistreated

The soul shivers on all you do,
For all the horrors you brew.
Awakened the dead from graves,
All those scars that you paved.

Hear that scream, their lurid cry,
You can't clutch that burden even if you try.
Still they long to live through,
They care for you besides your shrew.

You won't even dare to peek inside
In that hollow unspoken fears reside.
Just gaze those eyes filled with tears,
Please man, fear no one, but fear whom all
fear.

Desire

A day I wish to stand solitary,
Stand part from world's misery.
Away from the earth, beneath sky,
Neither moreover low, nor excessively
high,
Glancing at enormous hills,
Probably empty spaces might fill.

Moving as a lonely cloud,
There're million things to feel proud.
I want to be conscious, still lost,
Far away might stand a land coast,
All that I dream, wishing on shooting star,
Loosing hope with dead soul par by par.

Just a step and a deep breath,
Deciding to be angel or a Seth.
For every choice there's an outcome,
Life was not ever a song to hum.
As though I was careful on choosing
steps,
I should have watched before I leapt.

Silence

I couldn't dare to gaze into her eyes
That reveal pain behind, silent disguise.
Those petals lock unspoken falling out,
Can't imagine of battles you've fought.

Within that stillness, I can hear ample
words,
That unfortunate soul sensed all sort of
absurd.
For once that broken silence hit so hard,
Your verses stole away part of my heart.

You spell out nothing, still declare so
much,
Felt grieve, pain...flow of words touch.
That soul's so innocent, so very clear,
I would love to feel all your fears.

Life Phases

Pain only chooses those worth it,
Happiness, sorrows don't watch profit.
Tears fill the eyes, yet never shed
The surfs of gloom over the sea bed.

Can I once bring back time I've lost?
I tried to escape, but it made me its host.
We are characters on stage of life,
Fighting a battle against time to survive.

Though as sand, it slipped off my hand,
Cruelness and misery rules our land.
We are travellers with no place to stay,
Through those hardships, we still mend the
way.

Slight Favour

Please doesn't scratch on unhealed
wound,
I tried to plant happiness; let it bloom.
Eyes never drizzle, yet heart bleeds,
You think I am unaware, but I heed.

I am still lost, though I walk with crowd,
Inside I roar…never scream out loud.
I ignore my feeling, still it hurts.
Then hiding it all, laughing I revert.

I never asked a favour, now I do ask,
For my heart not abides to be sorrows
cask.
Why don't you understand my reality
differs?
I will never nature myself as you prefer.

Hypocrite

World seems as huge barrel of sorrow,

If only spoken words let the spirit harrow.

For great deeds do turn into weeds,

Then instead on emotions they feed.

Righteous path was full with thorn,

Erase all fake faces you've worn.

You hide that light, let it glow,

Reveal that kindness hidden in burrow.

You lie all around but lies benefit never,

It leaves scars unhealed forever.

You play dirty tricks to let others down,

For time brings back everything back around.

Maybe I can

I can never grasp stars in palm,
Yet I believe to touch the sky.
I walk with all the people on land,
Yet I believe one day I'll soar up high.

I can't breathe in waves forever,
Yet I believe to swim in depths inside.
I can't ride over the mountains,
Yet I believe to touch its peak, keeping fear aside.

I can never fly with wind far away,
Yet I believe to dance as it blows,
I wish to hold the time but can't, even if I may,
Yet I believe enjoying each second as it flows.

I wish to stay with whom I want forever,
Yet I believe everyone bids goodbye.
I can't hold the tears in eyes,
Yet I know the heart stops bleeding never.

Think about it...

Might it be easy to walk barefoot on coal?
Besides, destroying already destroyed soul.
Eyes were once mirror to heart,
For what would you see if you tear it apart?

If you were burdened with what you plot,
You'd died suffocating with its bloat.
Similar land, similar roof for beings to live,
Won't it be better besides hatred, love you
give?

But blood runs thin in those vessels,
Why should you care, why not easily
hustle?
It's not your pain not your grieve,
Then bother for what, why for right heave?

Avenged Lady

Is she the same girl I used to know?
Who used to laugh and waddle with the
flow,
I see she's loosing herself somewhere,
For we know life never plays fair.

Once I used to feel alive, when she was
around,
But now she's forgotten how to fly off the
ground.
I just desire to gaze inside her soul,
Steal away all the sorrows that she holds.

She still giggles, hiding her fears,
For none ever noticed eyes filled with tears.
I see her alone even in everyone's presence,
Dash the memories of bitter past and race
with present.

Feel the Unsaid...

Sometimes silence speaks unsaid words,
Even those that were once upon unheard.
The tongue doesn't retain any bone,
Still can grow wild plant where flowers
were grown.

They hide so much, and then what do they
reveal,
For life's not an agreement, why make a
deal.
They wear one and only mask for each day,
Hunting each day, making feelings their
prey.

We are all responsible for all that we do,
I just wish wounds were external-easy to
sew.
Wish to escape, sometimes want to avenge
But for definite peace is better than
revenge.

New Year

Left behind the disappointments.
unpleasantness of past,
Waiting desperately for enchantment this
year would cast.
Perhaps life will be poles apart or possibly
remain the same,
Absolutely uninformed either to win or lose
the game.

Prepared to battle whatsoever comes
forth?
This is perfect time to build a happiness
fort.
Just have faith, time would reveal its truth
as it slips,
Thenceforth you would be left with
harmony or maybe whips.

Watch Your Steps...

I have so abundant to say, but the voice
shivers,
I was certainly not at this juncture to be a
pain heaver.
Sometimes I think people understand the
silence,
But all this stage, I had been in ignorance.
This world is occupied with cunning,
masked walking heartless,
Never understood their lives properly and
made world a mess.

They hold a grudge meant for not one
confident cause,
You have moved out so far,

Maybe it's time to take a pause.
Just give a glance to all

You planted in the period departed,
You sowed the hatred, but never realized
what you parted.
At this time, the minute you are tired,
hopeless and weak,
Today you are left all alone, Nobody
around to hear you squeak.

Perfect as You are

Some people change because they need
importance,
They assume it's meant for better, but are
you aware.
What I contemplate, you are in ample
inadvertence,
Your innocent voice unexpectedly turned
into thunder blare.

Stand facing the mirror,

Intend to look into your eyes,
Can you see the same person hidden behind
the mask?
Every night a new-fangled soul is born and
old one dies,
I know it's not the one, I know it's time to
unmask.

Your brain is a factory of ideas, But it's you
to choose,
I believe your decision would be for finest
ending.
Too kind to listen to people but better to
follow personal views,

Good times to reveal all the truth, stop
pretending.

It's certainly not immoral to be the one who
you really are,
No one on earth possibly will do your part
as you play.
Please come back home for you haven't
travelled far,
Nobody's faultless, best in their weird ways
for all made of clay.

Broken down by Loved Ones...

At midnight stood, beneath the tree, observing clear sky,
Splashing water with feet, reflecting the divine moon light.
Quite place, no voice, no noise, Suddenly I heard a cry,
Skinny old lady in bitter cold, O, what a terrible sight!

Walked towards her, sat alongside and questioned,
But ears couldn't accept her miserable reply.
Abandoned by the one she raised, Ah! New era's fashion,
Once on whom all were dependent has nobody beside to rely.

Deprived from shelter and dying from starving,
Uh! What a ransom for nurturing a child who come to be an adult.

The one, their passport to world is
struggling for surviving,
Men, just fear truth, time will reveal soon
you were such a colt.

Humanity

I've no time to standstill and explore,
The ship of life had struggled hard to reach
shore.
Sometimes I wake up in dark...sweat
running down,
Miserable fears and nightmares made me
drown.

Then I see a hand trying to help me
through,
Let go off the qualms that once grew.
I try to reach and grab it greatly tight,
Unexpectedly from dark someone brings
me to bright light.

I stare hardly enough to know the
aforementioned exists,
But after helping me, it vanishes into
mist.
For benevolence never needs a reason to
feast,
Turns a man into human that once
remained a beast.

Vicious Memories

I held onto his hand to never let go,
So late to realise he wasn't a friend but
foe.
He stabbed my heart tremendously hard,
Amazing at using gentleness as his fad.

Never thought to encounter someone that
cunning,
From all those wounds still running.
Walk on earth still feel like walking on
shattered glass,
Left me with nothing but just coarse
memory crass.

My soul slowly recovers, but again when I
think,
World goes upside down within a wink.
Tried to make escape, leave all behind,
But can't kill thoughts travelling through
my mind.

Captured-Part (I)

Words under no circumstances speak;
actions certainly reflect,
For each step taken ensures noble or
remorseful effect.
As night falls in despair, left completely
single-handedly to suffer,
World is too inhuman, occupied with
people who never think what they utter.
They prove themselves to be truthful,
masking veiled tales,
None to blame but thyself...In silence their
dishonesty gales.
They cut off her wings so under no
circumstances might she soar again,
From all the agonies and dreads this
woman hid her in imaginable secret den.
Bleeding and wounded, severe pain
surviving with untreated scars,
Tried to overcome fighting to escape and
run missing some place far.
Battling with her own self, would she ever
or not ever flourish,
A day she might bloom, stand one in
millions as Flores.
Hope could undeniably dwell even if
entire world's in despair,

Ups and downs come and pass away,
have plenty of time so why not prepare.
Sun—a fiery ball, blazing and mighty, but
sets as soon as the time moves close,
Just a right day, right place and chance,
the whole world will stand to applause.
She's been chained, hand tied together,
left to die within a dark room,
Nothing ever takes breath away more
rapidly than the gloom.
Killing her everyday yet doesn't agree to
remain below any charge,

How extensively would you be successful
to keep her away with barge?

Captured Part (II)

She once thought wishing on a star was
truth, but it's just fairy tales,
Too foolish to keep expectation, part of
flesh resting in rib cage easily frails.

Storm of memories, flooding thoughts
with no dead end, no escape,

Don't let them draw, don't let them
mould; I deny to be the way they shape.

Take away the breaths; snatch the soul,
grab as hard as you may well,

For maybe you are uninformed, precious
pearl always grows in a shell.

Hold her wrist, feel the heat, hold it so
tight so you can feel the beat,

Just hope you might find an exit from this
illness of self-conceit.

She holds right to choose her way; stop
marking the start and ends,

Stop being her enemy if you can't be kind
enough to be a friend.

Nor complaints, neither grudges, just a
humble and polite request,

Let this girl fill the pages herself, for it's
not yours but her test.

Bleeding Heart

She scratched herself extremely hard for
she couldn't bear the mental pain,
That girl tried to protect herself but nothing
helped, not even saint.
Hid her in darkness so none would ever
understand what lies inside,
She pretended to waddle from place to
place, keeping her dreads aside.

She learned a lesson, for none ever rise
until they have been through fall,
That girl would never let anyone enter for
just harshness had resided the heart walls.
The time she was all by herself no one put
forth his hand except god
He always replaces the remains of heart
that were once torn

UMBER PERVAIZ

Yes, I call Myself a Human

Yes, I call myself a human

For one drop might not matter much

We only weep when harshness touch

We feel the slightest things that happen

We try to steal others' right, Why so raven?

Yes, I call myself human

Yes, I call myself a human

We live with others, still plot against our brothers

Love to put ourselves first, Still boost we care for others

We stare at all that happen, Still remain ignorant

We would have never found a hideout if our thoughts were transparent

Yes, I call myself a human

Yes, I call myself a human

We burden ourselves with tons of things

We learn to raise everyday even if you cut
off our wings

You brew soberness still we find our way
to bliss

We put others into certain category as we
wish

Yes, I call myself a human.

My Story...

Don't read my story when you are
unaware what's written on pages, I had
perfectly played my role, Though it was
hard to act in those stages.

They are still ripping my flesh, digging a
tunnel through my bones,

They can't imagine how dreadfully I've
been hurt from all thrown stones. I never
wish to erase, for what's written thought
me so much;

For every word, sentence and all the verses
make me woe as I touch.
Most of the pages are blank, waiting to be
filled with bliss or gloom,

For the pages will never end until I live;
They'll just keep on filling an empty room.

Bitter or Better...

I am not a shadow; don't suppose me to
follow your footsteps,
I consider thinking million times, for I may
collapse if I leapt.
I fear sorrows with sudden boom, life forced
me to gloom,
Still I hide within swallowing nightmares,
giving bliss some room.

This is the only life; no sir, I have no
additional lifespan,
For life is just a bitter poison that we and
ones before drank.
There's an easy course, yet I choose to drive
through rough path,
I might breakdown more or may build up by
something that it hath.

Young Love (1)

Hear her cry in the darkness of night,
For yet, moon's not ashamed to give her light.
Wet cover reveals her tale every morning,
She remains wide awake, though all snoring.

Doors remain shut, windows wearing silk garments,
For wall's hiding her away with candle its ornament,
But though in silence, one day she heard a song,
Bhe could now hear her heartbeat, it's been so long.

Undressed the window to look for the owner of that
voice
Who made her stoned heart melt into ice,
A young lad leaning on tree, stood still till horse
graze,
All that she could do for now, stand before and
gaze.

Unknown Fear

I doth feel so much, yet little do I say,
What hath been planted on the way.
This world's too small, yet troubles are
great,
All that I can do is to patiently believe in
fate.

What else could go wrong, stuck already
in storm,
Well if this is the act then, I am ready to
perform.
I am quiet but can't stop the waves and
tides,
Let's just walk and uncover what
darkness hides.

Alive Am I

I have lived a million times, and so have I
died,
I have lived in ignorance, and so have I
been guided.
I have lived in peace, and so have I felt
pain,
I have lived with lost soul, and so have I
with gained.

I have lived with wonders, and so have I
with mysteries,
I have lived in present, and so I have in
histories.
I have lived with eyes closed, and so have
I with open,
I have lived mended, and so have I been
broken.

Blind Truth

For they think I tell a tale,

No sire! My words hide hidden meaning,
For everyone's playing mind games, Then
whom are you believing.
For if life was just a fantasy, Probably we
would have lived it better;
For maybe things we think don't matter,
would have mattered.

For we simply believe, wish gets granted
wishing on a star,
For we still get scared when someone
promises to walk with us that far.
For I know it's hard to trust blindly, but you
are aware nothing's forever,
For neither are we fools, yet nor are we
extremely clever.

Dark End

There's just another door; I knock on it
every day,

Yet I hear nothing what it wants to say,
Does it warns me of the fear, Something
that might break me on the way.
My heart's already shattered, Broken bones
with flesh ripped off,
Within a bunch of nasty people, Can't
reveal the pain but just buff.

Meet my own self every day,

When I lie on the floor watching the clear
sky, They never know the presence,

But once you travelled far, Nothing but cry.
The tank of patience is too full, It demands
to burst, please don't pour too much!
I am completely disabled, too hopeless—

Not even able to cover distance with crutch.

Fine art

Too cold, too dead; oh no! I touched my heart,

Too late to hold on, I have already fallen apart.

They speak about the journey, nobody mentions fear,

The path has twists, girl; it's not as it appears.

Don't look too deep, there's an empty space,

Just look from above, never try reaching the base.

Don't think she will battle no sire, she forsake to attack,

There're already holes in walls, Don't forget to fill cracks.

Wish there was a lullaby,

So in slumber remain forever,

But whosoever made the first song was extremely clever.

They say look for the moon so you fall
amongst star,

What if she tells you don't live for minutes,
just live for hours?

If...

If only once you understood, Things I
meant to say,
If only once you understood,

My heart dying day by day.
If only once you understood, Time never
would remain the same,
If only once you understood, Humans are
never meant for tame.

If only once you understood,

My thoughts that I never convey,
If only once you understood,

The world I observe my way.
If only once you understood, Perhaps the
choices would change,
If only once you understood, Maybe
everything wouldn't seem so strange.

This is How it Goes....

Just look back and take a glance,

Left with regret for a missed chance.

Wings couldn't always take you at height,

The one who's not valour can't be a knight.

Even the sky seems to bow if you look to the ends,

Still the human ego—stiff as the mountain stands.

Some flowers bloom in the sunshine, yet some are fond of darkness,

Be it the bravest of all, yet all have a weakness.

Shut the eyes to all that you see, still can't stop the heart to feel,

Seems impossible but the one giving wound could only help to heal.

It may seem strange, but that's how it
goes,
Everything has to set that once rose.

UMBER PERVAIZ

Masked Beasts

Speak a little, little do
say,
Free today, but tomorrow's prey.
Hide the truth or hide from truth,
Believe yourself, yet not the youth.

Comfort is less, though the pain's more,
Bitter fruit dipped within sour.
Darkened room, just a ray of light,
Life's sweet, bitter, sour cake, Just take a
bite.

Build with clay, a small journey but long
way,
It's never forever home to stay.
Do good, for good passes hand to hand,
If you can't build, don't destroy
motherland.

Truth About life

If I was to make a fine escape, I would go
somewhere and never return,
What if I have lost all the chances?
Someday it would be my turn,
On a single tree blossoms bloom, Some too
early yet some late,
Some say everything's in our hands,

Some say just believe in fate.

If getting what we want was so easy,

Then the whole world would have stepped
on moon,
But believe me, everyone out there,

Not every child born holds a silver spoon.
Trees stands tall, yet the force of wind
makes them bow,
For the ones on earth could harm you as
much as you allow.

The boats were always meant for sailing in
the sea,
But don't forget a small seed soon turns
into a huge tree.
There is a reason behind everything that
occurs, either it might be unexplainable,

You don't need a huge rock to break the glass, but just a small pebble.

Bad always Comes with Hidden Good

Rush towards happiness, then why don't
you run for pain?
Cry for what you had lost, then why don't
you weep for gain?
Could easily learn to hate, then why don't
you learn to love forever?
Assume world's full of fools, then why do
you call yourself clever?

Is this what We Are?

This life is too small, so give it your all,
For you and I are actors playing different roles,
Raise yourself up high to the sky,
Let the world remember you even if you die.

Breath to live, don't let the life take breadths,
Search for the goods, don't fear the depths.
Hold on tight, for there's too long flight,
Let's look for treasure hidden beyond your sights.

Free yourself for your soul needs rest,
Choose what's right or either choose what's best.
Discover where you belong before it takes too long,
If you don't think me to be right, then why do you consider me wrong?

Tales of Times

There comes a time of tales that shatter
your world for a while,
This world is not a place of peace, in silence
rests the wild.
Erase the scars of the past, but don't forget
what you learned,
There rests a road to take you ahead, but
loved ones don't forget the turn.

If the lines on palm described destiny,

Just think cutting off would change what's
forth,
No sire, you don't mean too much, For the
evil beast, you are of no worth.
Just walk with me and hear what I say, I
hold mysteries on the go,
The sky shivers and the earth cries for
hidden truth you never know.

UMBER PERVAIZ

Lost Days

Feel the pain; no sire, no more!
Every second's getting day by day sour.
It's running as I never planned,
Time is slipping off my hand.
I stand here with bundle of regrets,
And though I try, yet never forget.

Soon there'll be a chance to make amend,
Broken hearts will somehow mend.
I can't breathe anymore, I am drowning,
Yet no response, but just frowning.
Was it my fault, or was it you to blame?
For if this is stage, than play a fair game.

Mystery of Bones

For she's a flickering flame, Don't touch, let
her burn,
Don't try to be her master,

For what you know she already learned.
She's a fire holding a heart so dead, so very
cold,
For it would take a little longer for wounds
to heal that are too old.

Neither a burning sun or a shining moon,
She is just the bright sky of noon.
Fighting soul with bag of bones,
How would the world be like if you had
own clones?

Masked Beauty

Love the thousand stars, so as they fill the
sky,

But don't forget there is moon that gives
them its light.
Love the wind that blows,

But don't forget the silent danger that is
invisible to human sight.
Love the tress that stand tall, But don't
forget the deadliest and beautiful creatures
they hold.
Love the water waves,

But don't forget they cause disaster if
strongly they rolled.

For beauty comes with danger and flaws,
There even resides monster with no huge
jaws.
Life is a mirror; reflect as angel or a Seth,
For if you wish to live happily, If you believe
in life after death.

What if each deed done caused a mark on
your face?
I bet you won't find any hiding place.
If you can't walk on footsteps of the ones

who were right,
Kill the demon inside you, it's your own
fight.

Unknown Myth

Life is a myth—an unknown tale,

Beautiful song of a nightingale.

Silent breeze with millions echoes,

Plenty of thorns on the stalk of rose.

Rowing boat with chances to float or sink,

Be wise to think, past and future have some link.

Hollow trunk could grasp so much more,

Empty well can't be filled no matter what amount you pour.

Wandering Still

Some questions should not be asked,

Without a masquerade, they are masked.

Footsteps cannot be counted when the road
goes long,

There's always something good behind
every wrong.

Voices need not be loud, just a whisper's
enough,

All paths not smooth, some need to be
rough.

Fall as much as you can, so you learn to
rise,

They say wise doesn't commit mistake, is he
really wise?

A tale just need words to spread, Need not
to be real,

Dreams are not dreamt from running time
you need to steal.

Be like water standing still or one that
flows through hills,

It's not the bravery, but yes, the cowardly
definitely kills.

Variations

Do all words that we speak always make sense?,

Even though you say truth, others take as offense.

Maybe I am in an illusion that things would be way I plan,

All may vary even though they were clans.

UMBER PERVAIZ

Change before Change

I don't hear the leaves rustle; no sire, no more!

Living in the world of silence, what for?

Stars that used to twinkle once simply disappeared,

Hold your hand when you're strong, leaving you alone in fear.

Demanding others to be honest, dipped within lies,

Loved one time never stops, just in a blink it flies.

Speak when you know the words hold meaning,

Trying to dust others' house while own not cleaning.

Bonds of Love

I thought my actions were strong enough to let him know what I feel,

It's always easy to give great wounds, yet always hard to heal.

Tsunamis never destroy you, Questions are daggers even worse,

If I couldn't be your angel,

At least don't let me be your curse.

I might wander the whole world, But my destiny leads me to you,

If you doubt the whole world, Never doubt the love so true.

I would never promise a garden of happiness, nor bunch of pain,

Think my love to be just, yet people who love are never sane.

If waves could measure the extent, I will ask them to spread far,

The depth of our love would even fade the brightness in cluster of stars.

Your arms are the only home where my
comfort resides,

The bond between our soul, the place
where peace hides.

River of Time

Either ways you turn hour glass, sand loses never,

No matter how much you heal wounds, scars remain forever.

You hold a book of blank pages, write whatever you will,

Pour water wherever you wish, it never rests still.

Think thoughts, dream the dreams, don't demand to fulfil.

Heart beats the same way, yet feelings always differ,

Dear one, it's all round, sometimes comfort, sometimes suffer.

Tell me white lies with million shades, shades I may not know,

Everything stops at one point, no matter how fast it may fro,

It all comes back, think wise what away you throw.

Live for What You may…..

I am a shadow; can be seen, never caught,
Leaving footsteps on every corner of
motherland,
Looking for precious treasure, what
treasures to sought,
Desire money, precious things or love; do
desire what,
Breath is never promised forever, it's
slipping off hands as sand.

May my ego reach the sky,

Just a second and there I bid goodbye.
All was sent here, yet never promised an
eternal life to ply,
Will be gone as a passing wind, just wish
someone would sigh.
Why regret when something's gone, Just
treasure till you hold on.
Wish the heart was good enough the way it
kept hate,

It forgave.

Petals with Thorns'

I thought the love would be same,
For there would be no fears to tame.
Just thought there won't be lies,
Just thought my souls would no longer
fright.
Would it be good enough if you knew me
little more?
Though you might never understand what I
did, what for.

Yes, I fear not the truth but the masked
lies,
Just if you knew truth is bond, Just strong
knot that two tie.
May you live in your fears,

Don't judge what you may not know,
Let the heart love you for you, Don't Force
hatred to grow.
Just if you asked, why would I not offer you
my soul?
Why would I blame an innocent? When the
one I trust is foul.

Fool to be Wise

They say not to teach the wise, Don't you
realize he's still learning,
Don't try to throw water in that flame, the
one constantly burning.
Walk on the rhythm if you don't understand
the notes,
For if you can't trust your plans, believe on
what destiny plots.

Trust your reflection, for shadow may leave
you when in darkness,
For never give the same back, if you are
treated with harshness.
World is beautiful place filled with terrors
and adventures; Explore,
If you need to be heard, don't squeak, roar
as lion roars.

Fight of Survival

Travel the world, for may you know what
you not,
You've been given an empty bucket, it's you
to sought.
Honour your self-respect, don't encourage
self-satisfaction,
Spit words, they echo back and never turn
into actions.

Breeds of different kinds, races to be better
than one another,
Physical killing's considered crime; how
about emotional murder?
The wounds bleed, yet the blood doesn't
appear,
They promise to be there in darkness, at
time just disappear.

Bloom in the Darkness

How long do you think holding yourself
back would help?
Would it be wiser to let the person feel the
same way you felt?
Sometimes all that you need is just a small
confession,
You yourself are responsible for being in
that progression.

They can captivate you, yet can't cut your
wings,
Don't wait for someone to show you light,
choose what life brings.
Few plants even survive, no matter in what
situation throughout the year,
They deal bravely with all come across
nonetheless what they bear.

SOLDIERS

Rest in peace, O beloved one,
For no one cares you are tomorrow's rising
sun.
They carry bloody corpses each day,
No one's there to hear their silent pray.

Innocent minds, innocent hearts lie ripped
and torn apart,
For social status matters more, Walking
dead with stone heart.
None bother as you not so close so dear,
Be proud, you lose life in battle field; they
die each day with inner fear.

Drive through Edge

No one knows where to begin, yet none
discover where to end,
It's a simple life; stay awake, Don't ride it
through the bends.
Walk straight with heads up, Little
stumbled, stop and hold,
Yet an additional day, discover strong suit
you behold.

Sweet ones don't hide behind a night and
shining armour,
For a foolish man may not be fool; May he
be wiser far more.
Act when you be acquainted with how one
would react,
World is round; personal reflection is what
you at all times attract.

Homeless

For they hear nothing, but yes, I hear her say,

People are just travellers, some visit and some stay.

Mankind is nothing but a hollow piece of creation,

Yet so loud, dismissive, evil, rude and impatient.

She sings a lullaby for her young ones to sleep each night,

Fighting a battle that she wasn't meant to fight.

Feared, hungry and homeless is this all they receive.

For if you cannot provide better, what they own don't seize.

UMBER PERVAIZ

Trickster

Oh sir, did I step on that painful nerve?

I believe you should have known this is
what you deserve.

Plot as you may, for don't think who would
you come across,

There's always a boundary I believe you
ought not to cross.

A sign is enough for a wise to learn what
he's been thought,

Yet, if you choose ignorance, prepare for a
battle never fought.

Don't dare to awaken that hidden beast,

It's beyond your imagination on what it
would feast.

Treachery is a form of art for a sinful being,

Let me open up your mind; trust me, it's for
your well-being.

Warning is all that can be given to the one
who seeks,

Don't fall into devil's pit, what he shows is
merely nothing but foul tricks.

Inner Bliss

Just glance the way she walks at the shore
of the sea,

A wise beautiful maiden would you just
wait and see.

Who could have ever thought in this world
full of mystery?

She stood to follow her heart and fled
away so free.

No wonder I would like to hear what she
has to say,

For she seems so full with joy, finding her
own way.

I see her gather herself together and walk
away so peacefully,

For she has learned the art of true
happiness and reflects it so gracefully.

Gratitude

Work a little harder, it's all that they say,

Well, dear sir, I am losing all that hope day
by day.

All that I see is people filled with greed,

For when there's God's wrath, Where would
you heed?

If you come across good, though go on to
seek better,

Then why do you complain when your
dreams scatter?

Be content with what you have been
blessed,

For he knows what's best for you, Why are
you so obsessed?

Polished Stones

Not all is royalty with a jewelled crown,

Don't label people white, black and brown.

Lend a hand, whenever asked for,

Let your kindness be louder than a lion's roar.

For I see the future in the sparkling little eyes,

I know he wins a battle, the one who tries.

We are present, the ones went were past,

So be sure to do good, as it's what the future would cast.

Character

Sing to the rhythms of the song,

They say don't think what is right, what wrong.

Keep it as it serves your purpose,

Well they pretend to be a joker in a circus?

If you can't fill a blank paper with some sense,

Won't you be titled a fool, why do you take it as offense?

Dig deeper for further something you might discover,

For if you haven't seen hatred, you will never be a lover.

Memories

Would you stop, would you hold on if I ask to let go?

I am trying to catch the moments, though the time loves to flow.

For a blossom blooms beautifully, yet take a look at the top,

There stands a lonely one looking out for some hope.

Step ahead, further more! Beware there's more trouble,

Well if you would be wise enough, life's nothing just a puzzle.

Put all the pieces in order for a picture might itself reveal,

Yet if you walk away, don't leave your sign, for the wounds need time to heal.

www.ingramcontent.com/pod-product-compliance
Lightning Source LLC
Chambersburg PA
CBHW061252140726
47998CB00006B/2205